FEB 0 5 2004

W9-AMQ-593

Illustrated by
Robin Lee Makowski

Published by Rourke Publishing LLC
Copyright © 2002 Kidsbooks, Inc.

Printed in the USA

Rourke Publishing LLC
Vero Beach, Florida 32964
rourkepublishing.com

Makowski, Robin Lee
Cats / Robin Lee Makowski, ill.
p. cm. – (How to draw)
ISBN 1-58952-152-8

INTRODUCTION

This book will teach you how to draw many different types of cats. Some are more difficult to draw than others, but if you follow along, step-by-step, then (most importantly!) practice on your own, you'll soon be able to draw all the cats in this book. You will also learn the methods for drawing anything you want by breaking it down into basic shapes.

The most basic and commonly used shape is the oval. There are many variations of ovals—some are small and round, others are long and flat, and many are in-between. Most of the figures in this book begin with some kind of oval. Then, other shapes and lines are added to form the basic cat outline.

In addition to ovals, variations of other basic shapes, such as circles, squares, rectangles, triangles, and simple lines are used to connect the shapes. Using these basic shapes will help you start your drawing.

Some basic oval shapes:

SUPPLIES

Soft Pencils (#2 or softer)
Soft Eraser
Fine-Line Markers
Drawing Pad
Colored Pencils, Markers, or Crayons

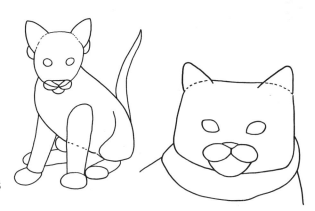

HELPFUL HINTS

1. Following steps 1 and 2 carefully will make the final steps easier. The first two steps create a solid foundation for the figure—much like a builder who must first construct a foundation before building the rest of the house. Next comes the fun part—creating the smooth, clean outline drawing of the animal and adding all the finishing touches, such as details, shading, and color.

Note: Following the first two steps carefully will make the final steps easier.

2. **Always keep your pencil lines light and soft.** These "guidelines" will be easier to erase when you no longer need them.

3. **Don't be afraid to erase.** It usually takes a lot of drawing and erasing before you will be satisfied with the way your drawing looks.

4. Add details and all the finishing touches **after** you have blended and refined all the shapes and your figure is complete.

5. **Remember:** Practice Makes Perfect. Don't be discouraged if you can't get the hang of it right away. Just keep drawing and erasing until you do.

HOW TO START

Look at the finished drawing of the Siamese below. Study it. Then study the steps it took to get to the final drawing. Notice where the shapes overlap and where they intersect. Look for relationships among the shapes.

1. Draw the oval for the head shape first. Then draw freeform shapes for the chest and body and connect them to the head, forming the neck. Using simple shapes and lines, add the ears and facial features. Sketch additional shapes for the legs and tail.
Remember to keep these guidelines lightly drawn.
2. Blend and refine the shapes together into a smooth outline of the cat's body. Keep erasing and drawing until you feel it's "just right."
3. Refine the features and add outlines for the patterns of color on the face and legs.
4. Carefully sketch in the dark and light fur lines. When you're satisfied with your drawing, you may want to color it.

Siamese cats have tan or cream-colored fur with darker color on their face, tail, legs, and paws. These dark areas are called "points." There are four kinds: blue point, lilac point, chocolate point, and seal point.

Sometimes it's helpful to start by first tracing the final drawing. Once you understand the relationships of the shapes and parts within the final drawing, it will be easier to draw it yourself from scratch.

Erasing Tips
••• Once you have completed the line drawing (usually after step #2), erase the lines you no longer need. Then proceed to refine your drawing, adding fur, shading, other details, and coloring.
••• Using a permanent, fine-line marker over your pencil guidelines will make it easier to erase the pencil lines.
••• A very soft or kneaded eraser will erase the pencil lines without smudging the drawing or ripping the paper.

Remember: It's *not* important to get it perfect. It *is* important for you to be happy with your work! Use your imagination and create different objects and backgrounds to enhance your drawings.

Most of all, HAVE FUN!

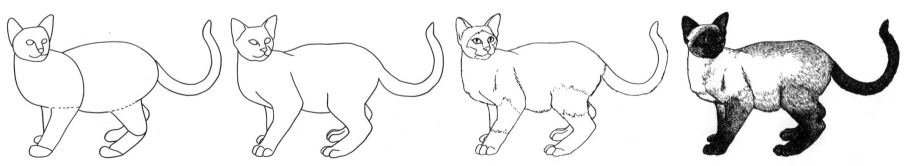

1.   2.   3.   4.

Sphynx

Sphynx cats have such short hair that they look hairless! They are affectionate and get along well with other pets.

Note: Always draw your guidelines lightly in steps 1 and 2. It will be easier to erase them later.

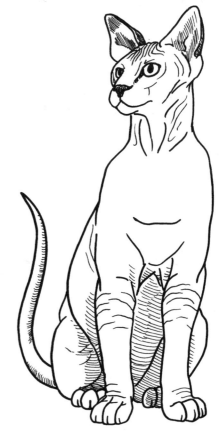

2. Blend the shapes together into a smooth outline, erasing the lines you no longer need. Refine the facial features and add the toes.

3. Draw the head, neck, and leg wrinkles. Darken the nose and lightly shade in the ears and lower body.

1. Begin by sketching an oval-shaped head. Add the ears, eyes, and muzzle. Sketch the free-form shapes for the chest and body. Don't forget to add the legs, paws, and tail.

Coloring: The Sphynx can be white, black, tan or gray.

Angora

This breed of cat originated in Turkey. Angoras are intelligent and make loving and devoted pets.

1. Start with an oval-shaped head and add the large free-form shapes for the chest and body. Add the guidelines for the small triangular ears, facial features, legs, and bushy tail.

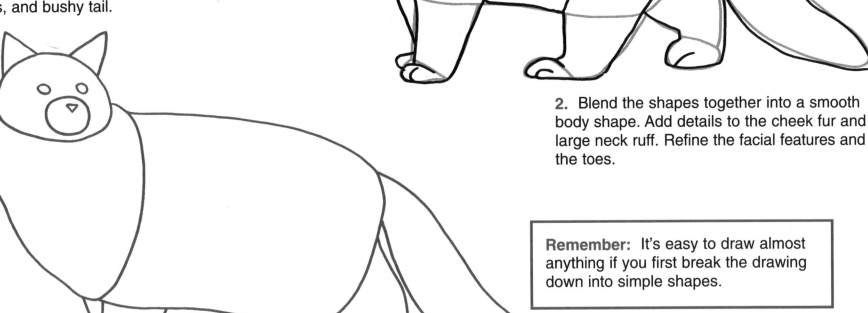

2. Blend the shapes together into a smooth body shape. Add details to the cheek fur and large neck ruff. Refine the facial features and the toes.

Remember: It's easy to draw almost anything if you first break the drawing down into simple shapes.

3. Use short strokes to make the edges of the fur fuzzy. Further define the facial features.

4. Use long strokes to add the fur. Keep the patches on the head, chest, and legs white. Don't forget to add the whiskers! Complete your drawing by adding the finishing touches.

Coloring: Classic Angoras are white, but Angoras can be any color.

Tortoiseshell

The name tortoiseshell refers to cats with random patches of red, black, and cream.

Note: It's easy to draw almost anything if you first build a good foundation.

1. Sketch an oval shape for the head. Add the round muzzle, eyes, and the triangle-shaped ears. Draw the free-form shapes for the chest and body. Add the long tail and paws.

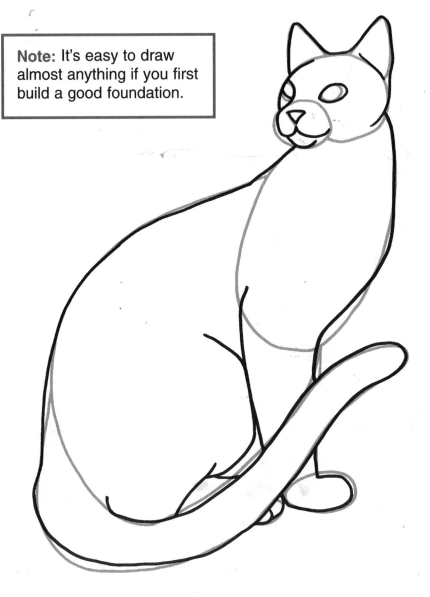

2. Blend the shapes together, erasing the lines you no longer need. Shape the muzzle, eyes, and ears.

3. Sketch the patches on the face and body, as shown. Darken the eyes and add the toes.

4. With a marker, use short strokes to add the fur pattern to the patches. When you have one layer stroked in, go back and add a few darker lines throughout the patch to complete the pattern. Leave the rest of the cat white.

Coloring: The Tortoiseshell pattern can be shades of black, tan, rust, and brown. In a number of breeds, the pattern can cover the whole cat.

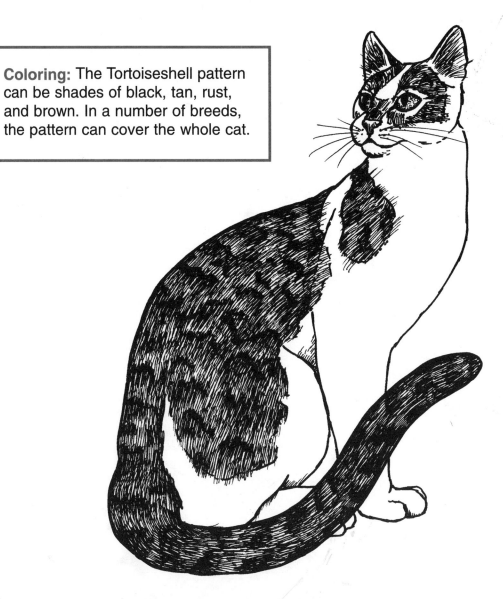

Turkish Van

This breed comes from Turkey. Turkish Vans are affectionate and love to play. They also like to swim.

1. Start with a diamond-shaped head and add the eyes, nose, and pointy ears. Sketch free-form shapes for the chest and body. Add the legs and the large bushy tail.

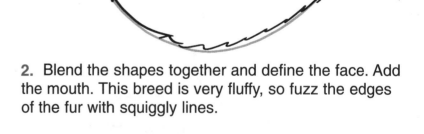

2. Blend the shapes together and define the face. Add the mouth. This breed is very fluffy, so fuzz the edges of the fur with squiggly lines.

Note: Take your time doing steps 1 and 2. If you get the basic foundation right, the rest of your drawing will be easy to draw.

3. Refine the facial features, adding the eye slits and the two patches above the eyes. Draw the paw pads on the bottoms of the feet. Continue to fuzz the fur.

4. Use long strokes to add fur on the body and tail, and use shorter strokes on the legs and face. Darken the paw pads and add whiskers to complete your drawing.

Coloring: Turkish Vans are white with orange ear fur and tail fur.

Devon Rex

This rare and unusual cat comes from England and has curly fur.

Remember: Always draw your guidelines lightly in steps 1 and 2. It will be easier to erase them later.

1. Sketch an oval for the head. Add the eyes, muzzle, and the triangle-shaped ears. Draw a free-form shape for the body. Add the legs and the tail.

2. Blend the shapes together and erase the lines you no longer need. Define the facial features.

3. Continue to refine the ears and facial features. The Devon Rex has a short, curly coat that waves in layers. Create the fur using short strokes on the face and body as shown. Don't forget to add the toes.

4. Continue to add the fur details using short, tight strokes. Darken the nose and ears and add the finishing details. Now this cat is ready to play!

For coloring: The Devon Rex can be almost any color or pattern.

Siamese

Popular, blue-eyed Siamese cats have tan or cream-colored fur with a darker color on their face, tails, legs, and paws. These dark areas are called "points." There are four kinds: blue point, lilac point, chocolate point, and seal point.

1. Lightly sketch the oval head. Draw the eyes, nose, and mouth. Add the large pointy ears. Sketch free-form shapes for the chest and body. Add the legs and the long tail.

2. Blend the body shapes together. Refine the head and face and draw in the toes.

Remember: It's easy to draw almost anything if you first break the drawing down into simple shapes.

3. Use fuzzy lines to create the pattern on the face, legs, and tail. Darken the eyes. Add the fur detail on the body and face as shown.

4. Use heavy strokes to shade in the dark area, but use light strokes for the lighter patches. Add the finishing touches to complete your sketch.

For coloring: The Siamese is a cream color with dark brown points (face, ears, tail, and legs) and crystal blue eyes.

Russian Blue

This elegant shorthaired cat has long slim legs, which are slightly longer in the back than in the front. Russian Blues are good natured and intelligent.

1. Draw a square shape for the head, and add the ears and facial features. Add free-form shapes for the chest and body. Sketch the legs and the long tail.

2. Combine and round out the shapes into a smooth outline of a Russian Blue, erasing the lines you no longer need.

Remember: Keep all your lines and shapes lightly drawn.

3. Refine the ears and face, add pupils to the eyes, and sketch in the pattern on the face and body. Lightly fuzz the fur as shown. Add in the toes.

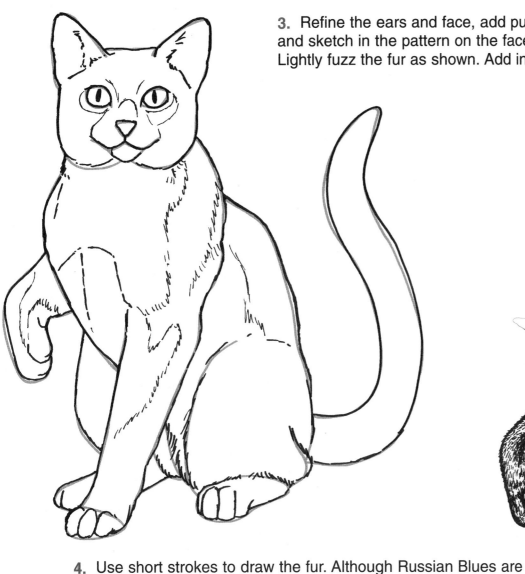

4. Use short strokes to draw the fur. Although Russian Blues are typically a bluish gray, your drawing will look more realistic if you leave some lighter areas in the fur. Darken the eyes and the nose to complete your drawing.

American Shorthair

American Shorthairs are large, usually friendly, and gentle cats. Their good nature makes them popular pets. Their fur can be any color or pattern.

1. Sketch a heart-shaped head. Add the guideline shapes for the eyes, muzzle, and then draw the pear-shaped chest and the free-form body shapes. Add the hindquarters, legs, and tail.

2. Refine the eyes and muzzle as shown. Combine all the shapes together into a smooth outline. Add the paw pads on the two hind legs and toes on the front paws.

Remember: Keep all your lines lightly drawn until you get to the final stages.

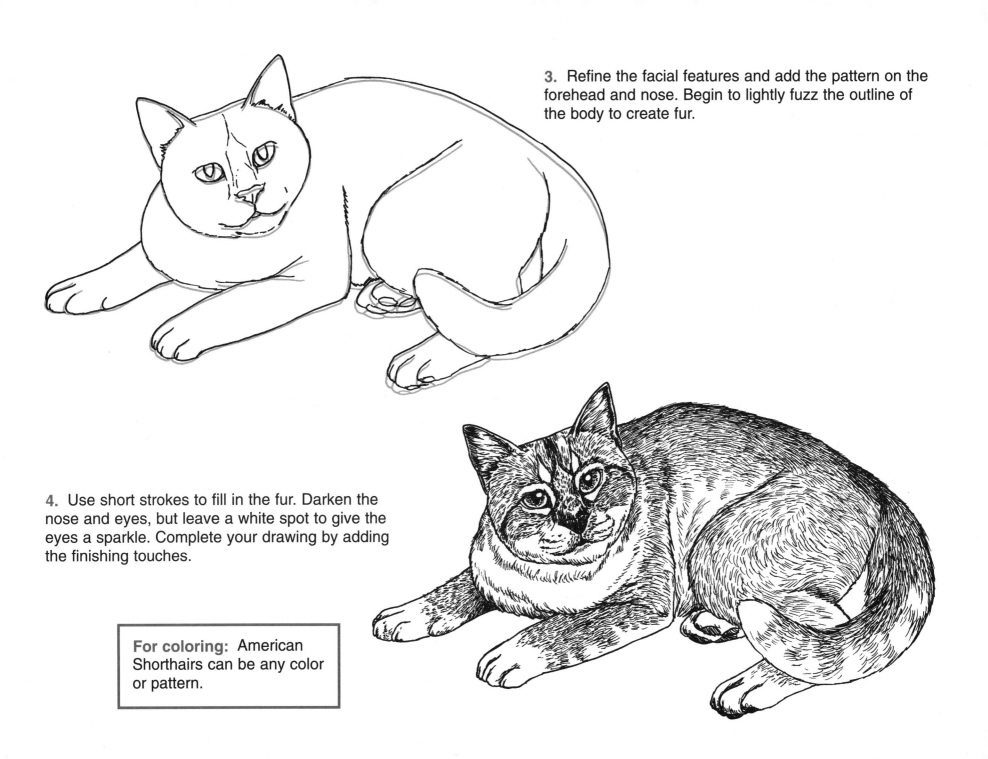

3. Refine the facial features and add the pattern on the forehead and nose. Begin to lightly fuzz the outline of the body to create fur.

4. Use short strokes to fill in the fur. Darken the nose and eyes, but leave a white spot to give the eyes a sparkle. Complete your drawing by adding the finishing touches.

For coloring: American Shorthairs can be any color or pattern.

Tabby Cat

"Tabby" refers to the markings on the cat and not the purity of the breed, as commonly believed. Stripes are the main coat pattern among these cats. Tabbies can be any species.

1. Begin with a large oval for the Tabby's face. Add the eyes, nose, and mouth shapes. Sketch in the large ears, and add lines for the neck.

2. Shape the facial features as shown and add the pupils. Lightly fuzz the outline of the head.

3. Draw in the pattern of stripes on the face and neck. Darken the outline of the eyes and pupils.

4. Use short and heavy strokes to fill in the dark stripes and lighter strokes for the other areas. Add in the whiskers and other finishing touches to complete your drawing.

For coloring: Tabbies can be many colors, but the characteristic that makes them "tabbies" are the shapes of the stripes.

Maine Coon

Maine Coons are gentle creatures and get along well with children and other pets. They enjoy playing in the water.

1. Start with large ovals for the head and chest. Add the facial features and remember to add the pointy ears. Sketch in the body, leg, and tail.

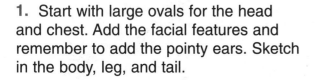

2. Blend the shapes together and refine the face, erasing any unnecessary lines. Lightly fuzz the ears and the neck ruff. Add the toes.

Remember: Always keep your pencil lines light and soft so that the guidelines will be easier to erase when you no longer need them.

3. Add the stripes and other markings to the face as shown. Darken the outline of the eyes and add the pupils. Use long and short strokes to fuzz this cat's fur.

4. Use long, loose strokes to fill in the fur. With a marker, darken the stripes on the face. Add the whiskers and your drawing is complete.

Coloring: This Maine Coon is rust, tan, cream and white with black markings. Maine Coons can be any color.

Persian

This longhaired Asian cat is famous for its long, fluffy fur. It has a round face, round eyes, snub nose, and small ears. Persians come in many different colors.

1. Start with a large oval for the head and chest. Add the guideline shapes for the facial features and ears. Draw the football-shaped body. Add the legs and the large bushy tail.

2. Blend the shapes and erase the lines you no longer need. Define the facial features. Fuzz the bottom of the neck ruff and tail. Add the toes.

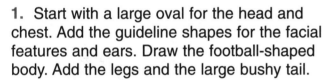

Hint: Don't be afraid to erase. It usually takes lots of drawing and erasing before you will be satisfied with the way your drawing looks.

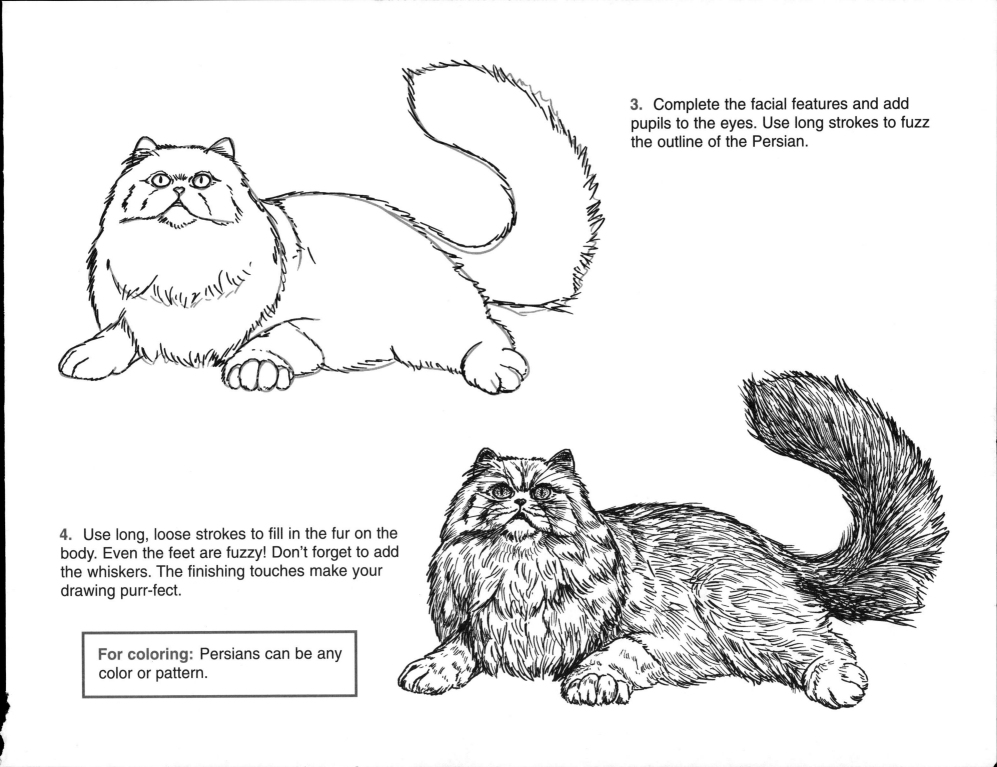

3. Complete the facial features and add pupils to the eyes. Use long strokes to fuzz the outline of the Persian.

4. Use long, loose strokes to fill in the fur on the body. Even the feet are fuzzy! Don't forget to add the whiskers. The finishing touches make your drawing purr-fect.

For coloring: Persians can be any color or pattern.

Calico

A Calico cat has irregular patches of black, orange, and white-colored fur. This unusual-looking cat can be either a shorthair or longhair.

1. Lightly draw the oval-shaped head. Add the ears and facial features. Sketch the free-form shapes for the chest and body. Add the leg and tail.

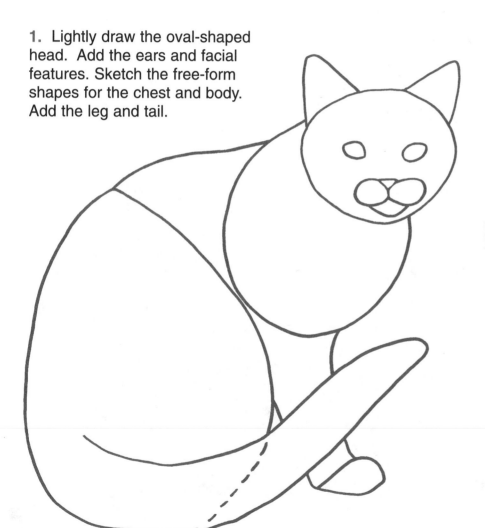

2. Blend the shapes together, erasing the lines you no longer need. Refine the facial features and add the toes.

3. Complete the face and begin to add the Calico's distinct pattern on the saddle, tail, and face.

For coloring: Calico cats are white with black, cream, tan, and reddish splotches on their back, head, back legs, and tail. The splotches are not "brindled", or mixed up.

4. Use heavy strokes to fill in the dark patches and light strokes for the other areas. Leave the neck ruff, chest, and paws white. Darken the eyes and add the whiskers.

Abyssinian

Each hair of an Abyssinian's fur is several different colors. It starts out silvery, then gradually changes from brown to black.

1. Begin with an oval for the head, and add the eyes, ears, and muzzle. Sketch a free-form shape for the body, adding the legs and the long tail.

2. Blend the shapes together and erase the lines you no longer need. Define the facial features and draw the pupils. Add the toes.

Note: Make sure you have built a solid foundation with the first two steps before going on to step 3.

4. Use light, short strokes to fill in the fur detail. Use a heavier stroke on the neck and tail patterns. Add the whiskers and other final touches and this Abyssinian is ready to meow for you.

For coloring: Abyssinians are slender cats and can be any color, but the markings are consistent in all members of the species.

3. Sketch in the pattern on the face and darken the eyes. Add the pattern on the body as indicated. Lightly fuzz the ears.

Puma Cub

Pumas are also known as cougars, panthers, and mountain lions. A cub's dark spots and tail rings will disappear before it becomes one year old. Cubs can be easily tamed.

1. Start with a big, egg-shaped face. Add in the bullet-shaped ears and the two little half-circles underneath. Sketch the free-form body shape. Add the big, thick legs and the thin tail.

2. Blend the shapes together. Define the ear shapes and the other facial features, and add the toes.

3. Sketch in the spot pattern and markings on the face and body. Don't worry, they don't have to be exact. Add the claw sheaths on the toes and pupils in the eyes.

4. With a marker, use squiggly lines to fill in the spots on the face and body. Use short strokes to fill in the fur. Add the whiskers and other finishing touches.

Coloring: Puma Cubs are tan with black and white markings.

Remember: Always feel free to use your imagination when adding the final touches.

Longhaired Silver Tabby

This spectacular-looking cat has a clear silver undercoat with black tabby stripes on top. The stripes are slightly blurred due to the extra-long fur.

2. Use short strokes to create fur for this tabby. Add the pupils and darken the outline of the eyes. Refine the shape of the muzzle and nose.

1. Begin with a square-shaped head. Add the slanted eyes, nose, and muzzle. Draw the small triangular ears. Sketch in the neck ruff.

3. Use long, loose strokes to detail the fur. Darken the nose and add the whiskers. With a few finishing touches, your portrait is complete.

For coloring: The Silver Tabby is silvery gray. You can use light blue and lavender for highlights and shading.